To Rab
Best wishes for Christmas 2006

POSITIVE THINKING FOR
CALVINISTS

Also by Ian Black

WEEGIES vs EDINBUGGERS
MERR WEEGIES vs MAIR EDINBUGGERS
CATS vs DOGS
MEN vs WOMEN

POSITIVE THINKING FOR
CALVINISTS

THE SCHOOL OF SOFT KNOX

IAN BLACK

BLACK & WHITE PUBLISHING

First published 2005
by Black & White Publishing Ltd
99 Giles Street, Edinburgh EH6 6BZ

ISBN 1 84502 079 0

British Library Cataloguing in Publication Data:
A catalogue record for this book is available
from the British Library.

Printed and bound by Nørhaven Paperback A/S

Calvinism is the belief that there are three Gods. That good works, or the love of our neighbour are nothing. That faith is everything, and the more incomprehensible the proposition, the more merit in its faith. That reason in religion is of unlawful use. That God, from the beginning, elected certain individuals to be saved, and certain others to be damned; and that no crimes of the former can damn them; no virtues of the latter save.

Thomas Paine

The covenant of life is not preached equally to all, and among those to whom it is preached, does not always meet with the same reception. This diversity displays the unsearchable depth of the divine judgment, and is without doubt subordinate to God's purpose of eternal election. But if it is plainly owing to the mere pleasure of God that salvation is spontaneously offered to some, while others have no access to it, great and difficult questions immediately arise, questions which are inexplicable, when just views are not entertained concerning election and predestination. To many this seems a perplexing subject, because they deem it most incongruous that of the great body of mankind some should be predestinated to salvation, and others to destruction. How ceaselessly they entangle themselves.

John Calvin (Institutes III.xxi.i)

INTRODUCTION

Those among you who have read Bill Duncan's *The Wee Book of Calvin* may have been struck by the excellent quality of the writing, as was I, but what exercised me most was the philosophy offered. I recognised almost every mean-spirited and dark-souled saying and aphorism as something that I had heard or had preached at me in the kirk or classroom and I got to wondering why, if I grew up in the same repressed and depressed cultural matrix at the same time as him, how come I am such a cheerful, optimistic wee bastard? One who has never bought a self-help book in his life.

My conclusion was that there are millions of Scots like me. Take the Tartan Army, for instance. What other country has such a collection of headbanging, cheerful optimists, urging their team on against all odds and all previous experience? And there are lots of other for instances. Laughter in the face of adversity is one of Scotland's best traits, admired everywhere in the world. We didn't invent black humour, but by God are we good at it.

So this is a kind of counterblast against, as Calvin's chum John Knox might have put it, the Monstrous Regiment of Pessimists and Doom and Gloomsayers who try to poison our society and our individual lives with their constant drip of sneers, scorn and self-righteousness. As we say in Glasgow: 'If your life is so shit, get a helmet, okay.'

The words within these pages will help, I hope, provide an

umbrella against the drizzle of pessimism, a barque to carry you through a sea of troubles, a levee against the pent-up waters of resentment of other people's success and happiness. You may think that you have to put up with po-faced joy-killers averring their belief in a predestined universe with rubbish like 'Whit's fur ye wull no go by ye', whereas the truth is that your life will be so much better if you believe that whit's fur ye wull go by ye, unless you're quick and/or smart. Remember that wool grows just as fast on lazy sheep and for-bye, hard work sometimes pays off in the future, but laziness works right this very minute.

It is time to be positive. Buy this book and God will like you.

Fuck the begrudgers, son, for theirs is not the Kingdom of Heaven.

Robert S. Black, engineering storeman, philosopher, and father of the author

ADULTERY, HELL,
FOUR QUESTIONS AND AN ANSWER

Question

When you return to your house after a useful day's toil and you discover your minister on the kitchen floor shagging your wife, should you:
A) Shoot him.
B) Shoot her.
C) Shoot both of them.
D) Say to your wife: 'Arch your back, woman, and get the meenister's balls off that cold floor.'

Answer

D is obviously the answer as he is a Calvinist and therefore can do no wrong, at least in his own eyes, and as a bonus you will no longer have to endure his hours of ranting from the pulpit about the sin of adultery and the fires of hell while he is staring meaningfully at you and his wife.

FAT, OLD & HAIRY

Which is the worst type of Calvinist?
A) Fat
B) Old
C) Hairy
D) Related.

The answer is D, as I am all of the other three.

TRINITY

God and Jesus went to visit Andy Goram at his home. He invited them in, poured them a drink, got out the crisps and they settled down for a chat about Calvinism. There they were, seated around the table, The Father, The Son and The Goalie host.

JESUS CHRIST

And a Calvinist joke. Yes, there is one, even if I had to make it up.

When is the only time you hear the words 'Jesus Christ' in the Unitarian Church?
A) During the hymns.
B) During the prayers.
C) During the sermon.
D) When the beadle stubs his toe.

AGNOSTIC

Agnostic
Can God make a rock too heavy for Him to lift?

Calvinist
The question is irrational, counter-intuitive and absurd. I love it.

HELL

Question

If the Calvinists' God is omnipresent, that is to say, in all places simultaneously, where does He go for His holidays? Is it:

A) Millport.

B) Majorca.

C) Hell.

D) Calvinists? Holidays? Does not compute.

Answer

The answer is C, as where else would He get all those ideas for making people's lives a living hell?

LET THERE BE LIGHTBULBS

Question How many Calvinists does it take to change a light bulb?
Answer Change?

Question How many Calvinist TV evangelists does it take to change a light bulb?
Answer One. But for the message of light to continue, send in your donation today.

Question How many Calvinist fundamentalists does it take to change a light bulb?
Answer Only one, because any more might result in too much cooperation.

Question How many Calvinists does it take to change a light bulb?
Answer None. God has predestined when the light will be on. Besides, Calvinists don't change light bulbs. They simply read the instructions and pray that the light bulb will be one that has been chosen to be changed. And it is not going to matter to you if it does, as you are condemned to eternal darkness anyway.

THE RCM

The Righteous Calvinist Meenister (The RCM) is visiting the home of a parishioner whom he suspects might be up for a wee bit of backsliding, and they are having a stroll round the garden, which is a perfect example of what gardens should be – a riot of colour, scent and beauty. The RCM says: 'This is a fine spot, Hamish. Between your hard work and the grace of God you have created this heavenly haven on Earth.'

Hamish has a long look at the RCM and says: 'God and me together is it, Meenister? You should have seen it when He had it to Himself.'

When it gets dark enough, you can see the stars.

YET ANOTHER CALVINIST JOKE

What is a priest?
Someone who is called 'Father' by most children,
except his own, who call him 'Uncle'.

QUESTIONS, QUESTIONS

There are no really simple questions. Problems require thought and dedication.
But there are simple answers. There are just no good simple answers. Although that God one was pretty good for a while there.

CALVINIST ANSWERPHONE

At the tone, please leave your name, number, and a brief justification for the ontological necessity of modern man's existential dilemma, and we'll get back to you.

If you are one of the Chosen.

BUSINESS

The Calvinist business is a cruel and shallow pool of hard cash, an unforgiving and hallucinatory highway where thieves and rogues run free and good men die like dogs.
There's also a negative side.

*The one sure thing that we can be
certain of is the need for doubt.*

The secret of success in Calvinism is sincerity.
Once you can fake that you're laughing.

Faith can move mountains.
Just imagine what knowledge could do.

LIE

Calvinists: the truth is out there.

Hiding from you.

*Hope is the feeling you have that
the feeling you have isn't permanent.*

There's always an easy solution to every human problem —
neat, plausible and wrong.

We must believe in luck.
How else can we explain the success of those we don't like?

LORD GOLF ALMIGHTY

The Calvinist minister had two passions in life – the Lord and golf. After a very busy week when he had had no time for golf, he awoke early on a glorious Sunday morning. Of course, the only respectable things for him to do on the Lord's Day were to give the service, attend to the sick and persecute unbelievers. But the sun was shining and the golf course beckoned. After much wrestling with his conscience he thought to himself: 'Ach, it's so early, nobody will be about and I'll make the sermon double length to make up for it.'

As he heads to the golf course, St Peter rushes up to God and says: 'Master, don't you see yon minister heading for the golf course on the Sabbath?' Says God: 'Don't fret, Pete. He'll get what he deserves.' So Peter sits back and waits for a bolt of lightning to strike the unsuspecting minister. Instead he watches aghast as the minister hits the best round he's ever had, ending with a stupendous hole-in-one at the 18th. 'Master!' Peter cries. 'What are you doing? Why have you let him hit such an incredible round? I thought you were going to punish him!' Says God: 'I have punished him. He's just hit the perfect hole-in-one. Who is he going to tell?'

HUMOURLESS DOG

Chesterton said: 'It is the test of a good religion whether you can joke about it.'

Humour about one's religion arises when the group has sufficient confidence to both give and take mockery. Humourlessness correlates strongly to feeling threatened.
If, on appropriate occasions, the members tell, enjoy, and / or devise transgressively funny jokes about their denomination, it's a church.
If such jokes reliably and regularly meet with stifling social disapproval, it's a cult.

Calvinists, I rest my case, even if every dogma must have its day.

*There's nothing an Agnostic can't accomplish
if he really doesn't know whether he believes in it or not.*

Many Calvinists want to serve God,
but mostly only as advisors.

LET THERE BE MORE LIGHTBULBS

Question How many Calvinists does it take to change a light bulb?
Answer Two. One to put in the new bulb and one to paint it black.

And while we are on the subject . . .

Question How many Zen masters does it take to change a light bulb?
Answer None, for it is not the light bulb that changes, but your mind. And the mind does not exist.

And finally . . .

How many Luddites does it take to change a candle?

*The Lord didn't create anything without a purpose,
but midgies come damn close.*

Don't moan about your church.
If it was perfect, they certainly wouldn't let YOU in.

*A bigot is one who is obstinately and zealously attached
to an opinion that you do not share.*

God does not propose to judge a man or woman
until he or she is dead. So why should you?

The best way to cheer yourself up is to try to cheer somebody else up. This is very difficult in the north-east.

10 REASONS

This is from an American fundamentalist website, one of very few with a sense of humour. I haven't altered it at all.

10 REASONS WHY I AM A CALVINIST

1. Calvinists tend to wear wool and cotton. Dispensationalists tend to wear lime green polyester.

2. John Calvin was French . . . being French is very chic.

3. Calvin sounds like Calvin Klein . . . and his clothes are very chic.

4. Calvinists can drink.

5. Calvinists can smoke.

6. Dispensationalists are into prophecy conferences where they talk about Star Trek eschatology and the mark of the Beast. Calvinists have conferences on 'life and culture', art, social justice, and other high-

brow things like that. Afterwards, we go to the local pub and talk about philosophy over a pint of Bass ale.

7. Calvinists have close ties with Scotland and Scotland is very cool: you know – Sean Connery, the movie *Highlander*, bagpipes, the Loch Ness Monster, Glenlivet 18-year-old scotch, the movie *Trainspotting*, *Braveheart*, etc.

8. Calvinists think we are smarter than anybody else.

9. It is more socially acceptable to say, 'I go to Grace Presbyterian Church' than to say, 'I go to Washed-in-the-Blood Worship Center', 'I go to Sonlife Charismatic Believers Assembly', or to say 'I go to Boston Berean Bible Believing Baptist Bethel', or to say 'I go to the Latter-Day Rain Deliverance Tabernacle Prophecy Center, Inc.', or to say 'I go to the Philadelphia Church of the Majority Text', or to say 'I go to the Lithuanian Apostolic Orthodox Autocephalic Church of the Baltic Union of 1838'.

10. Ultimately, I am a Calvinist because I had no choice in the matter.

A NON-CALVINIST PRAYER

Lord, lead us not into temptation. Just tell us where it is; we'll find it.

NARROW OF SOUL

All of the Calvinists and others narrow of soul,
those people who would be enormously improved
by death, were called to be witnesses, not lawyers
or judges.

He deserves Paradise who makes his companions laugh.
The Koran

There is only one blasphemy,
and that is the refusal to experience joy.

HA!

If there is no God, who pops up the next paper
hankie in the box?

Monotheism is a gift from the gods.

VENGEANCE

Forget injuries, but only after they have been
avenged. Never forget kindnesses.

CHEER UP

One day as I sat musing, sad and lonely and
without a friend, a voice came to me from out of the
gloom, an ethereal voice, full of love and hope,
saying: 'Cheer up, things could be worse'.
So I cheered up and, sure enough, things got worse.

God could not be everywhere and therefore he made mothers.

God sells knowledge for labour – honour for risk.

Call on God, but row away from the rocks.

A heart in love with beauty never grows old.

If work were good for you, the rich would leave none for the poor.

In case of doubt it is best to lean to the side of mercy.

Live your own life, for you will die your own death.

Make happy those who are near, and those who are far will come.

The sinning is the best part of repentance.

What was hard to endure is sweet to recall.

When a blind man carries a lame man, both go forward.

When there is no enemy within,
the enemies outside cannot hurt you.

When you throw dirt, you lose ground.

Atheism is a non-prophet organisation.

Love of our neighbour is the only door out of the dungeon of self.

Be happy while you're living, for you're a long time dead.

Be slow in choosing a friend, but slower in changing him.

Fools look to tomorrow. Wise men use tonight.

Diplomacy is saying 'nice doggy', until you find a big stick.

Change in your life is inevitable, except from a vending machine.

CALVIN BECKONS . . .

You are perilously near to becoming a Calvinist if:

You enjoy talking to people in King James English.

You are building a pulpit for your living room.

You believe Moses should have shaved.

You have a picture of Sodom and Gomorrah, the day after they got it, and you look at it a lot and smile.

You scrawl bible verses on the bathroom walls of your local pub.

You thought *Back to the Future* was a movie about biblical prophecy.

You keep religious tracts in your mobile phone carrying case.

You can trace Saddam Hussein's genealogy to Nebuchadnezzar.

You think genuflect is a type of mirror.

You wish you could preach like Ian Paisley.

You know that 'Santa', unscrambled, is 'Satan'.

REQUIEM, YA DANCER

With all the sadness and trauma going on in the world at the moment, it is worth reflecting on the death of a very important person in May 2005.

Larry La Prise, the man who wrote the 'Hokey Cokey' died peacefully aged 93. The most traumatic part for his family was getting him into the coffin.

They put his left leg in, and then the trouble started.

TOP SHELF

The Calvinists have their own top-shelf magazines: *Prayboy* and *Repenthouse*.

THE FACTS

A Calvinist is a man who does what he thinks God
would do if only He knew the facts of the case.

Angels can fly because they take themselves lightly.

UNCO GUID

The unco guid should be aware that a halo has to
fall only a few inches to become a noose.

BORN AGAIN

Born again? Not me, pal. Pardon me for getting it right the first time.

SINNERS

Christ died for our sins, we are told repeatedly.
Should we make his martyrdom meaningless by not
committing them?

I'M A BELIEVER

If you are a believer then every night when you go to bed you should turn your worries over to God. He's going to be up all night anyway.

N B

Calvinists please note:
Few sinners are saved after the first 20 minutes of a
sermon.

FORGET IT

God isn't dead, he just has Alzheimer's Disease.
He's forgotten that we exist.

God often visits us, but most of the time we aren't in.

God will forgive you; He's in the forgiving business.

If absolute power corrupts absolutely,
where does that leave God?

If you want to be an atheist it's your God-given right.

If God lived on earth, people would break his windows.

LIFE ON EARTH

If God was condemned to live the life which he has inflicted on many of the people of this planet, He would kill himself.

OH, MISERY

If you get gloomy and depressed about the world's
miseries, just take an hour off and sit and think how
much better this world is than Hell. Of course, it
won't cheer you up much if that's where you expect
to go.

FIAT LUX

In the beginning the world was without form, and void. And God said: 'Let there be light'. And God separated the light from the dark.
And then did both washings.

ANSWER MY PRAYER

If you talk to God, you are praying. If God talks to you, you have schizophrenia.

Maybe there's no devil, it's just God with a drink in Him.

A LITTLE UNDERSTANDING

Most people are bothered by the bits of the Bible
that they don't understand. What bothers me is the
bits that I do understand.

NAE FUN

Calvinism is the haunting fear that someone, somewhere, may be having a good time. Real Calvinists put a stop to it.

BOOGIE NIGHTS

Why do Calvinists hate sex standing up?

They are afraid that it might lead to dancing.

ONE AT A TIME

Most sensible people are really all of one religion.
But sensible people never tell you what it is.

IMAGE RIGHTS

One can safely assume that you've created God in
your own image when it turns out that God hates
all the same people that you do.

THE GREAT 'I AM'

Hypothetical conversation between Descartes and
Buddha:

Descartes said: 'I think, therefore I am'.
Buddha replied: 'Think again'.

And while we're on the subject:

Descartes walks into a pub and the barman asks
him if he wants a drink.
Descartes replies: 'I think not'.
And disappears.

ZEN THERE WAS ONE

Question
What do you call a schizophrenic Zen Buddhist?
Answer
Someone who is at two with the universe.

And furthermore:

Two Zen masters walk into a bar.
Or do they?

Glasgow zen
It's aw wan, eh?

Happiness, freedom and peace of mind are always attained by giving them to someone else.
It is different with money.

*Give to someone without the expectation of a return,
and you won't be disappointed.*

We do not learn by experience,
but by our capacity for experience.

*Good judgment comes from experience,
and a lot of that comes from bad judgment.*

There's aye sorrow at somebody's door.
And happiness at lots of others.

Never draw your dirk when a blow will do it.

Don't marry for money,
you can borrow it cheaper.

DIFFERENT METHODS

Another Calvinist joke:

Question
How many Methodists does it take to change a light bulb?

Answer
This statement was issued: 'We choose not to make a statement either in favour of or against the need for a light bulb. However, if in your own journey you have found that a light bulb works for you, that is fine. You are invited to write a poem or compose a modern dance about your personal relationship with your light bulb (or light source, or non-dark resource), and present it next month at our annual light bulb Sunday service, in which we will explore a number of light bulb traditions, including incandescent, fluorescent, three-way, long-life and tinted, all of which are equally valid paths to luminescence.'

Lord, give me chastity and self-restraint,
but do not give it yet.

Virtue is its own punishment,
vice is its own reward.

Homosexuality is God's way of insuring that the truly gifted aren't burdened with children.

The Bible has six admonishments to homosexuals and 362 admonishments to heterosexuals. This doesn't mean that God doesn't love heterosexuals. It's just that they need more supervision.

If you think education is expensive, try ignorance.

*If you can learn from hard knocks,
you can also learn from soft touches.*

Experience is what enables you recognize a mistake when you make it again, so that you can do it with more finesse.

Always use tasteful words. You may have to eat them.

Wasting time is an important part of life.

Intel has just announced its new Calvinist chip: the Repentium.

Jesus saves! The rest of us better make backups.

Diet Commandment:
Thou shalt not weigh more than thy fridge.

Life is too short to drink cheap beer or grain whisky.

Eat properly, exercise regularly, die anyway.
Health is merely the slowest possible rate at which you can die.

Ministers are like nappies.
They both need changing regularly and for the same reason.

E H ?

And Jesus said unto them: 'And whom do you say
that I am?' They replied: 'You are the eschatological
manifestation of the ground of our being, the
ontological foundation of the context of our very
selfhood revealed.' And Jesus replied: 'What?'

LONG WEEKEND

God didn't create the world in seven days. He did a ghoster on the 5th, as He wanted the whole weekend off. This is why our Jewish cousins have their Sabbath on Saturday, as they have known this for ages.

NOW YOU SEE HIM

Jesus was a typical man. They always say they'll come back but you never see them again.

FINDERS KEEPERS

You found God? Hurray!
If nobody claims him in thirty days, he's yours.

Ambition is a poor excuse
for not having enough sense to be lazy.

If humanity was meant to use the metric system,
Jesus would have had ten disciples.

Quidquid latine dictum sit, altum viditur.
(Whatever is said in Latin sounds profound.)

If you don't pay your exorcist,
you get repossessed.

Quote from the Church of Elvis

Nobody ever grew despondent looking for trouble.

Eternity is a terrible thought.
I mean, where's it going to end?

War is God's way of teaching geography
to the people of the United States of America.

An unfortunate thing about this world is that the good habits are much easier to give up than the bad ones.

If you tell the truth, you don't have to remember anything.

Know thyself? If I knew myself, I'd run away.

Don't be so humble.
You're not that great.

PEES UND TOUCHHOLES

An old German proverb about predestination:

Alle Kunst ist umsunst Wenn ein
Engel auf das Zuendloch brunzt.
*All skill is in vain when an angel pees
in the touchhole of your musket.*

Priests who think themselves good at their job have an altar ego.

Never be afraid to try something new.
Remember, amateurs built the Ark.
Professionals built the Titanic.

Speak the truth, but leave immediately afterwards.

The way some people find fault,
you'd think there was a reward.

When you reach for the stars you may not quite get one, but you won't end up with a handful of dirt.

It doesn't matter whether you win or lose.
What matters is whether I win or lose.

Hard work never killed anybody, but why take a chance?

If a Calvinist and your mother-in-law were drowning, and you could only save one of them, would you watch the telly or just have a drink?

If ignorance is bliss, why aren't there more happy Calvinists?

As long as you've lit one candle,
you're allowed to curse the darkness.

As my grandfather used to say: 'If we all liked the same thing, the whole world would fancy your granny.'

Given enough time, what you put off doing today
will eventually get done by itself.

The road to Hell is paved with Good Samaritans.

*Immorality is the morality of those
who are having more fun than we are.*

WHY ELVIS WILL REPLACE JESUS

1. His motto 'Taking Care of Business' appeals to the power structure better than 'Jesus Saves'.
2. White jump suits are more practical than white robes in most parts of the world.
3. Elvis had better songs.
4. Elvis had sex.
5. Elvis approved of his followers having sex.
6. The Elvis Presley-Michael Jackson Estate will probably own most of the world anyway.
7. JC's disciples drove sheep; Elvis's disciples drove Cadillacs. Which would you rather be?
8. You don't have to starve yourself to emulate Elvis.
9. JC's followers learned 'turn the other cheek', Elvis's followers learned karate.
10. You're still reading this.

*It is easy to be wise. Think of something
really daft to say, then say the opposite.*

DO IT

It is the greatest of all mistakes to do nothing
because you can only do a little. Do what you can.
Do all the good you can, for all the people you can,
as long as ever you can.

THINK IT'S FUNNY?

Real intelligence requires both seriousness and humour. Seriousness without a sense of humour is a kind of stupidity. Humour without seriousness is another. Politicians, educators and religious leaders are usually subject to the first kind of stupidity. Those who take anyone in the first group seriously are afflicted with the second. Those in the first group seldom find anything funny. Those in the second group find everything funny, unless it requires them to think.

There is a difference between faith and superstition. What you believe is faith, what others believe is superstition.

Blessed are the flexible, for they shall not be bent out of shape.

We must believe in freewill. We have no choice.

When truth needs a voice, silence lies.

Thou shalt not be a victim. Thou shalt not be a perpetrator.
Above all, thou shalt not be a bystander.

There is no duty we so underrate as the duty of being happy.
By being happy we sow anonymous benefits upon the world.

*The disappearance of a sense of responsibility is
the most far-reaching consequence of submission to authority.*

If the concept of God has any validity or any use, it can only be to make us larger, freer and more loving. If God cannot do this, then it is time we got rid of Him.

Always do the right thing. This will please the people who are important to you, and, just as importantly, astound the others.

BOOKS YOU WON'T SEE PUBLISHED

Never Read a Bible Verse

Omnitemporality for Dummies

Why Reading is Killing the Church

Biblical Hermeneutics: You Can't Just Make Things Up

1001 Calvinist Jokes

Life consists of what you do, not what happens to you.
Things happen to a stone.

When you get to your wit's end you'll find
God lives there. And She'll still ignore you.

Peace starts with a smile, ya bastard.

IDEOLOGY AND RELIGION
– A COMPARATIVE GUIDE

Still confused? Here's a quick guide to who does what when the keech hits the rotary equipment.

Taoism
Shit happens.

Calvinism
Shit happens because you don't work hard enough.

Buddhism
If shit happens, it isn't really shit.

Zen Buddhism
Shit is, and is not.

Zen Buddhism #2
What is the sound of shit happening?

Altruism
Want some shit?

Confucianism
Confucius say – 'Shit happens.'

Hinduism
This shit has happened before.

Darwinism
We came from shit.

Darwinism #2
This shit was once food.

Islam
If shit happens, it is the will of Allah.

Islam #2
If shit happens, kill the person responsible.

Islam #3
If shit happens, blame Israel.

Islam #4
If shit happens, take a hostage.

Catholicism
If shit happens, you deserve it. It's your fault.

Protestantism
Let shit happen to someone else.

Presbyterian
This shit was bound to happen.

Episcopalian
It's not so bad if shit happens, as long as you serve
the right wine with it.

Methodist
It's not so bad if shit happens, as long as you serve
grape juice with it.

Congregationalist
Shit that happens to one person is just as good as
shit that happens to another.

Unitarian
Shit that happens to one person is just as bad as shit
that happens to another.

Lutheran
If shit happens, don't talk about it.

Fundamentalism
If shit happens, you will go to hell, unless you are
born again. (Amen!)

Fundamentalism #2
If shit happens to a televangelist, it's okay.

Fundamentalism #3
Shit must be born again.

TV Evangelism
Send us money and shit won't happen.

Judaism
Why does this shit always happen to us?

Seventh Day Adventism
No shit shall happen on Saturday.

Creationism
God made all shit.

Secular Humanism
Shit evolves.

Christian Science
When shit happens, don't go to a doctor – pray!

Christian Science #2
Shit happening is all in your mind.

Unitarianism
Come, let us reason together about this shit.

Quakers
Let us not fight over this shit.

Utopianism
This shit does not stink.

Capitalism
That's MY shit.

Communism
It's everybody's shit.

Feminism
Men are shit.

Feminism #2
That's not funny!

Chauvinism
We may be shit, but you can't live without us.

Commercialism
Let'™s package this shit.

Impressionism
From a distance, shit looks like a garden.

Idolism
Let's bronze this shit.

Existentialism
Shit doesn't happen; shit IS.

Existentialism #2
What is shit, anyway?

Stoicism
This shit is good for me.

Hedonism
There is nothing like a good shit happening!

Mormonism
God sent us this shit.

Mormonism #2
This shit is going to happen again.

Wiccan
And it harm none, let shit happen.

Scientology
If shit happens, see Dianetics, p.157.

Jehovah's Witnesses
Knock, knock
Shit happens.

Jehovah's Witnesses #2
May we have a moment of your time to show you
some of our shit?

Jehovah's Witnesses #3
Shit has been prophesied and is imminent; only the
righteous shall survive its happening.

Moonies
Only really happy shit happens.

Hare Krishna
Shit happens, rama rama, ding ding.

Rastafarianism
Let's smoke this shit!

Agnostic
Shit might have happened; then again, maybe not.

Agnostic #2
Did someone shit?

Agnostic #3
What is this shit?

Satanism
SNEPPAH TIHS.

Atheism
What shit?

Atheism #2
I can't believe this shit!

Nihilism
No shit.

Alcoholics Anonymous
Shit happens – one day at a time.

Environmentalism
You produce shit, so you have to eat it.

Socialism
Sorry, we are out of shit today.

Yoga
There's a full lotus shit happening.

Transcendental Meditation
Shit. Shit. Shit. Shit. Shit. Shit . . .

Vandalism
I'm going to break this shit!

Surrealism
Shit is shiny and shaped like a watch.

The Force
Do not be swayed by the Dark Side of the shit.

Shinto
Shit is everywhere. So as long as you're stepping in
it, show it some respect.

Dominicanism
Believe in shit, or we'll boil you in it.

Solipsism
All this shit is a creation of my imagination.

Spoonerism
Hit shappens.

Stalinism
The state treats you like shit.

Robinism
Holy shit, Batman!